For Mrs. Myers,
without whom this
story, and others,
wouldn't have
been told.

Byron
29 FEB. 2020
Wenonah

The Girl in the Haystack

by

Bryon MacWilliams

B.O.M.

Serving
House
Books

The Girl in the Haystack

Copyright © 2019 Bryon MacWilliams

ISBN: 978-1-947175-09-9

Library of Congress Control Number: 2018912693

Cover Design by Kristen Radtke

Serving House Books logo by Barry Lereng Wilmont

Published by Serving House Books

Copenhagen, Denmark, Florham Park, NJ

www.servinghousebooks.com

Member of The Independent Book Publishers Association

First Serving House Books Edition 2019

For Laura

Contents

Author's Note

This story was told to me, in conversations, by the woman who lived through it — as a girl — nearly eighty years ago. Voices are recreated, facts are not.

— B.D.M.

The Day After

My father is calling my name.

I say, "I'm over here!"

He walks over to me, stops, looks down. He's crying. He turns, calls my name again, walks away. He walks over, walks away, walks over. He won't stop calling my name.

"Here I am! Here I am!"

Wait. Why is a sheet covering my face, my body?

I can see the light bulb in the kitchen through the fabric. I can see my father.

Why can't he see me?

I try to lift my arm to pull aside the sheet but nothing happens, nothing moves.

Last night our neighbors, men, dragged my mother from the house into the dirt road. They kicked her and hit her with the fat ends of their guns. My older sister, Hanna, and I watched them do it. We stood in the doorway, screaming. When the men were done they walked back toward the house, toward us. Hanna pulled me away by the hand.

When I next opened my eyes I was on the floor, under a bed. My mother's clothes iron was under the bed, too. I reached for it, but my hand wouldn't move. I tried to crawl out from under, but my body wouldn't move.

Now I'm lying on my back on the divan and I'm covered by a sheet.

My uncle says from somewhere, "Let's help Pirl," my mother, "at least she's still with us."

Oh.

My Uncle Friedel thinks I'm dead. My father thinks I'm dead.

This isn't just a sheet, it's a shroud.

That's why there's something hard beneath my head — the Hebrew Bible, maybe, or a prayer book.

"Oh my God! I'm not dead, I'm alive!"

"Don't leave me. Don't leave me, alone."

I want to talk, but I can't. I want to move, but I can't. I can see, but no one sees me.

My name is Lyubov, but everyone calls me Lyuba. I'm seven years old. My name means Love in Ukrainian, but I'm not Ukrainian. I'm Jewish. My little town, Tuchin, was part of Poland when I was born. Then it was part of Ukraine, which is part of the Soviet Union, the empire. Now Tuchin is maybe part of Germany.

It is Monday, July 7, 1941, and I'm scared.

They want to bury me, alive.

Grandmother's House

Now I'm lying on a big bed — someone else's bed, in someone else's house.

I'm not covered by a sheet.

My eyes are so puffy I can barely see. My head feels big, soft.

My mother — I call her *Mameh*, or Mama in Yiddish — is on one side of me. Strips of cloth, brown red, are wrapped around her head. She keeps saying, "Please, God, take her, take her." She keeps saying it over and over.

My father, Isaak — I call him *Tateh* — is on the other side of me. He is calling me Lyubochka, not just Lyuba, and he is holding my right hand in both of his hands. I can't feel his hands on my hand, though. I can't feel anything on the right side of my body.

In front of me is a Ukrainian farmer, one of my father's customers. His name is Pavlo and he is handsome, with thick dark hair. Pavlo is standing, and crying. He keeps saying it's a miracle my mother and I are alive.

He shakes his head, "An absolute miracle."

Pavlo brought us milk, but I want an egg.

I can't talk, though, and my right hand won't move. So, with my left hand, I draw a kind of circle in the air.

4

Tateh thinks I want an apple.

But nobody knows what I want.

When the Ukrainians who call themselves *Bandérivtsi* came to our house they hurt Mameh and me, but they didn't hurt my sister. Hanna is three years older than I am. She has blue eyes and straight blonde hair. She looks Polish, maybe, or Ukrainian. But I don't.

I have hazel eyes and straight brown hair that Mameh braids. She ties the ends of the braids with red red ribbons.

When the *Bandérivtsi* came to our house — they were with a German soldier — Tateh was already hiding in the forest with other Jewish men and boys. Everyone knew Jews would be attacked after Germany invaded the Soviet Union.

The attack even has its own word — *pogrom.*

Mameh, Hanna and I didn't hide with the men and the boys because no one guessed the Ukrainian men would hurt women and children, too.

Mameh loves me, so she doesn't want me to suffer. She's praying for me. She's praying for me to die.

"Take her, God. Please, take her!"

5

Secret Places

Tateh keeps making places to hide in the house. It's our dream house — one story tall with red brick walls and a window of brightly colored glass in the front. We have four or five hiding places, already. The other day Tateh took off a board from the front steps, took out the nails, then put back the board.

It's been close to a year since the night of the pogrom and I can talk now, I can walk again. Every day Tateh massages my legs and my right hand, but three of my fingers still don't move.

Doctors won't come to help me or Mameh.

We don't have any medicine.

I feel safer in our house than in my grandmother's house — the house with the big bed, in the poor part of Tuchin — even though trucks carrying German soldiers, the Nazis, drive by all the time. When Hanna and I feel vibrations in our feet we know one of their trucks is coming, so we hide.

Mameh has been packing bags because today we're going on a trip. We can take some of our things, but not all of our things. I don't want to leave behind anything that's mine, though, not even the coats and dresses onto which Mameh has sewn yellow hexagrams, six-pointed Stars of David — one in front, above the heart, and one in back, behind the heart.

The word, *Jude,* is written in the middle of each star. *Jude* is German for Jew.

Today Tateh dug a deep hole in the dirt floor of the basement. He put a big pot in the bottom of the hole, then he put Mameh's gold and silver jewelry in the pot.

He told me and my sister to put something in the pot, too. Hanna put in her report cards from school. I put in my diploma —the one with pictures of Soviet leaders Vladimir Lenin and Joseph Stalin.

I also put my dolly in the pot. She has curly hair, and a pretty dress. I stood at the edge of the hole, held her out in one hand, and let go.

Then Tateh put a lid on the pot and filled in the hole with dirt. Then he broke out all the colored glass from the front window and nailed boards where the glass was.

The house is darker, now.

Tateh keeps talking out loud. He keeps saying this is it, this is the end — what happened in other towns is going to happen here, too.

We have all these places to hide, but nowhere is safe.

Before we leave for our trip there's a knock on the door. It's a man and his wife. They're from another country, Czechoslovakia. He's a school principal. Because they're new they don't have a place to live, so the Nazis told them they could live in any house owned by Jews.

When the principal and his wife see Hanna they ask my parents not to take Hanna with us — to let her stay behind, with them. They've always wanted children, they say, but they can't ever have their own. And Hanna is light-skinned and light-haired, like them.

My parents say no, never.

The principal says if Hanna stays, she might not be killed.

But my parents still say, no, and I'm glad — if we die, we'll die together.

You probably think it's weird that I talk too much about dying. But after the night of the pogrom, after I heard blood coming out of Mameh's head — it made a real sound, *zhhh, zhhh, zhhh* — I wasn't scared, anymore.

I didn't know I would stop being scared. It just happened.

There isn't any more room in our bags. Whatever we can't take with us will be someone else's.

I don't know where we're going. I just know things will be different, forever.

The Ghetto

People, just so many people, are walking in the same direction on the muddy road outside our house. Wherever there aren't people there are horses pulling wagons. The wagons are filled with wooden chests and rolled-up rugs and metal bed frames.

No one wants to let go of what's theirs.

Soon Tateh, Mameh, Hanna and I pick up our bags, follow the people. We follow them to the poor part of town. Jews from Tuchin, and near Tuchin, were ordered by Nazis and Ukrainian police to move into the same part of town, together.

It's both sides of a long road. How long? I don't know.

However big it is, it's called a ghetto.

In the ghetto there's a fence all around us — kind of like a wall, really. It's like we're trapped except there's a gate. We can go in and out whenever we want.

At my grandmother's house — she isn't alive anymore, Mameh's mother, but we still call her house her house — there's a big room with a small black stove and a chimney sticking out. All our relatives are here, except for Uncle Friedel, Mameh's brother. Last week he was arrested by the Nazis and hanged by the neck in the town square with nineteen other people, all Jews.

The house is so full. I don't even know how many relatives I have. On Fridays, before the sun goes down, my aunt washes the floors so they'll be clean for the next day, Saturday — the day that Jews rest the whole day. After she cleans the floors she covers them with newspapers.

She tells Hanna and me she'll break our legs if we mess up the papers.

If it weren't for Pavlo, the farmer, we wouldn't have any food. He brings us milk and eggs.

Tateh says we wouldn't have come here if we knew Jews were being moved into the same place so we'd be easier to kill.

When the Nazis chased away the Soviets, Tateh says, we could have run away, too — with the Soviets. But we've been living with Ukrainians for so long, he says, we thought Ukrainians couldn't live without us.

Jews and Ukrainians work together to turn trees into boards. We work together to turn animal skins into leather, for shoes, and to turn plants into cloth, for clothes. Tateh even sells seeds to Ukrainian farmers. Sometimes he gives money to the farmers until they can give it back.

We were wrong. Ukrainians can live without us.

They're even helping the Nazis find us and put us here, in the ghetto.

It's 1942, and now it's too late to run away. Now we don't have any good choices, Tateh says, only different ways of dying.

The whole time we've been in the ghetto the gate has stayed open. Today the voices from the loudspeakers on poles are saying the gate is going to be closed at three o'clock in the afternoon on September 24. That's tomorrow.

"This is truly the end," Tateh says.

He tells me to get Mameh out of bed, we're going on another trip. Mameh washes my hair, brushes it. Then she helps me put on a nice dress — one of the ones with the yellow stars.

No Jews are allowed outside without stars.

I don't know where we're going, but this time we don't pack any bags. Tateh, Memeh, Hanna and I walk through the gate, and along muddy roads, until we reach a river. It's called the Horyn' River, but I don't know why. On the riverbank is a rowboat. Standing around the boat are five or six Ukrainian boys — maybe twelve, maybe thirteen years old.

Tateh asks the boys to row us to the other side.

The boys aren't nice to us, but for money they say, yes.

We get into the boat. Then, in the middle of the river, one of the boys stands on the walls of the boat with both feet. He moves his legs so fast that the boat tips from side to side. The boat almost flips over.

"Maybe the stinking Jews need a bath?" he says.

I start to cry. I can't help it.

The boys laugh. They yell for more money, and Tateh gives it to them.

As soon as we get to the other side the boys jump out of the boat and run up the hill, yelling. They're yelling for the Nazis. Ukrainian police come, instead, and they push and punch Tateh. They won't let us walk anymore. Then a Nazi comes on a motorcycle. He points a small gun at us, makes us walk all the way back to the ghetto. He follows us on his motorcycle.

At my grandmother's house my parents decide to break their promise. They decide to let Hanna stay with the principal and his wife. If Hanna pretends to be their daughter, not my sister, she might not be killed.

I want Hanna to live but I can't help it, I tell her, "Hanna, don't go!"

She says, "I'm doing what our parents tell me to do."

And she does.

Mameh washes her hair, brushes it. Then Hanna leaves, just like that — walks out of the ghetto, with Tateh, wearing a pretty dress and ribbons in her pretty blonde hair

Hanna always does as she's told. She's the good one.

Not me.

I must be the bad one, I think. I must be the devil.

Just in Time

It's late afternoon in the ghetto, my big sister is gone, and too many noises are coming in through the window.

Pavlo is here. He says he heard we were stopped by the police this morning, near his farm. He has clothes from his wife and daughters. The clothes don't have yellow stars. If Mameh and I put on the clothes, he says, he'll take us with him — out of the ghetto, to his farm.

Just for a little while, he says.

Tateh nods.

Then Pavlo says he's sorry, but he doesn't have any clothes for Tateh. He says the Nazis would stop us at the gate, kill us all, if a second man tried to walk out of the ghetto with Mameh and me.

From now on Tateh will be on his own.

We tell Pavlo we can't leave, yet, that Hanna is coming to say goodbye before the gate closes at three o'clock tomorrow.

Pavlo says we can't wait, that the Nazis are going to close the gate even sooner, as a surprise.

Mameh and I go into another room and put on the clothes. When we come back Tateh gives Pavlo Mameh's gold watch.

Pavlo says he doesn't want the watch, but he'll hold it for us until we want it back.

When Mameh and I leave with Pavlo we aren't carrying anything, not even our own clothes. Well, the shoes are mine — leather boots made by a shoemaker in the big town, Rivne, boots with long laces and lots of eyeholes.

Everything else of mine is at my grandmother's, or in the pot in the dirt.

I hate leaving behind my things.

Mameh and I walk next to Pavlo. When we get close to the gate I'm nervous, but I'm not scared. Well, maybe I'm a little bit afraid. Afraid is different than scared. I'm afraid because I don't know what's going to happen.

No one stops us at the gate, though. No one even seems to look at us.

Once we're through, once we're on the other side, I can't help it — I look back. I see Nazis with machine guns standing near the fence. I see Ukrainians with empty sacks, waiting.

Waiting for what?

I think I know, but I'm not sure I know.

I just know something bad is about to happen.

Pavlo's farm is in the village of Shubkiv. It isn't far, but it feels far when you're walking in the mud, farther from your father, farther from all your relatives, farther from your house with the boarded up window and your only sister, pretending, inside.

At Pavlo's farm no one is home — not even Pavlo's wife, not even their son and two daughters. In the yard there's a dog, though. The dog is a boy, and he isn't big or small. He has a round chest and a small head with a big nose. He has short brown hair that is dark on his body, and light on his legs.

I look at the dog, and the dog looks at me. He doesn't move — he only looks.

I keep looking at the dog until Pavlo opens the door of his house. He lets in Mameh, then me. After he shows us to the attic, he leaves.

It's quieter on the farm than in the ghetto. But the next day we hear faraway noises — gunshots, lots of gunshots. From an attic window we see smoke and flames above the trees.

Tuchin is on fire, my mother says.

Is Tateh alive? Is Hanna still safe?

Dog Meets Girl

Yesterday I was just sleeping
under my plum tree, in my yard,
when my ears went straight,
and they twitched, and twitched
again, so I opened my eyes and saw
Master walking in really short steps
toward the house, and a woman
walking behind him, and a little girl
walking behind her, and the little girl
was holding the woman's hand,
but Master wasn't holding anyone's
hand, he just had his head down,
and the woman had her head down,
too, but the little girl had her head up,
and she was looking at me, so I looked
at her, and she just kept on looking
at me, so I just kept on looking at her,
but she didn't smile, so I didn't smile,
even though I love to smile, if you
really want to know, then Master
opened the door of the house
and held it open, the door, and
the woman walked in, and
the little girl walked in, and then
Master walked in, and the next time

the door opened Master came out,
alone, and even though I waited and
waited for the little girl she never
came out, Master just stood in my yard,
alone, then he walked over to me and
my tree and put a hand on my head,
just held his hand there, on my head,
and when I looked up he scratched
behind my left ear, softly, which felt
good but not as good as usual because
I just couldn't relax, which is my
favorite thing to do, if you really
want to know, but I just couldn't
relax because Master looked scared,
like how everybody looks scared
these days, except maybe for
the little girl. I love her. I just do.
I can hear them talking, the little girl
and the woman, from high in the house.
I've never been in the house because
I'm always just outside, watching.
Today there is a fire on the other
side of the river, I can smell it.

First Haystack

When I think about everything that's happened since the night of the pogrom it's like none of it has happened to me. It's like I've been reading it in a book.

Before the war we were happy. Everyone in the ghetto said we were. I knew that our babysitter, Anya, ate pork, and that no one in my family ate pork. But I didn't know that made us different kinds of people — just that she ate pork, and we didn't. Now I know that our neighbors, maybe even Anya, were ready to hurt me and my family, maybe even to kill us, because of what we eat.

Now I know that men hunt people like animals.

Now Hanna is living like an orphan with strangers from another country.

Now I never run to play but lace my boots in case I need to run for my life.

We used to hide in our house from Ukrainians who wanted to hurt us. Now we're hiding at the house of a Ukrainian who wants to save us.

I don't understand everything.

Tateh is on Pavlo's farm now, too. Can you believe it?

Mameh and I were so happy to see him. No one else was happy to see him, though.

Pavlo's wife — her name is the same as mine, but everyone calls her Lyubka — keeps telling Pavlo that by saving our lives he is risking the lives of their son, Mykola, and their daughters, Klavdiya and Halina. Pavlo's brother lives on the farm, too, but Pavlo can't even tell his brother about us because his brother would tell on us to the Nazis.

Actually, Pavlo wants us to leave.

He never planned on keeping us, my parents say. He just can't let us go.

We're not in the attic anymore.

We're inside a haystack, in a field.

Pavlo made a hole, we crawled in, and he covered up the hole with hay.

We never see the sun. We never feel a breeze.

The haystack is taller than my father, taller than two of my fathers. Most of the time we can't see, we can only hear. You'd be surprised how much we know from just listening.

Whenever we talk we whisper. And we don't talk at all when we hear the dog barking.

The dog's name is Brisko.

If it's safe, he's quiet. If it's not safe, he's loud.

That's how we knew the other day not even to whisper, not even to move a centimeter. Brisko was barking and barking, then a metal pole with a pointy end poked into our haystack. Brisko kept barking as the pole came in, then went out. Then it came in again, and out, scratching Tateh on the cheek.

The Nazis.

Tateh says other Jews must be hiding in haystacks, too.

That time in the attic, when Mameh and I saw smoke above the trees, it was the ghetto in Tuchin that was burning. We know because Tateh was there. As soon as the gate was closed — Pavlo was right, it was closed early as a surprise — some Jews set fire to houses near the fence. Then Jews with guns started shooting at the Nazis and their Ukrainian helpers.

People in the ghetto ran for the fence. Some climbed over, others pushed through. Nazis shot some of the people when they got to the other side of the fence, but not most of the people. Tateh, who isn't tall, climbed over the fence and jumped down on the other side — next to a Nazi with a gun.

The Nazi was looking away so Tateh ran past him.

Tateh says it was a miracle.

It was his fate to survive.

Most people ran into the forests, but Tateh ran to our house. He took off the board without nails on the front steps, crawled under the steps, then put back the board.

Later, when he heard Hanna outside, he called to her.

The fire burned for three days and nights. And for three days and nights there were gunshots. Every day Hanna took out food to Tateh — crusts of bread, whatever she could hide from the principal and his wife. The day she didn't come out with food Tateh knew it was time to leave, time to try to get to Pavlo's farm.

It was night when Pavlo brought him to our haystack.

Tateh says all our relatives in the ghetto are dead.

He doesn't have three sisters anymore.

But I still have my one sister.

I'm glad Hanna isn't in our haystack. She's in a better place — our house.

None of us were supposed to be alive, but we are.

More and More People

I smelled smoke for three whole moons,
and for three whole moons people came
to my farm, just so many people, and
all of the people, even the babies, were
quiet, they just came up the hill, quietly,
and moved across my yard, quietly, and
hardly any of the people looked at me,
they just moved into the trees, just
disappeared, but then more people came,
different people, no women or girls
or babies, just men and boys, with guns,
and they weren't quiet at all, and they
moved into the trees, too, so it was
just me again, alone, in my yard, and
I don't like being alone, if you really
want to know, even if I'm getting used
to being alone because only Master
leaves the house anymore, everyone
else just stays inside, even my little girl,
she's always inside a haystack. Is it
silly to love someone you've never met,
someone you've never even touched?

I never even see her, my little girl,
but I hear her talking with the man
and the woman, and I hear her stop
talking whenever there are gunshots
from the trees. Today women with babies
came out of the trees and moved down
the hill, quietly, toward the river.
Then men with guns came out
of the trees, behind them.
Master is digging in the barn.

Mice, Rats, Lice

Because we don't go anywhere, things come to us.

Mice come to us. And rats.

When Tateh gives me a piece of bread I hold it in the hand that closes all the way, my left hand. I make a fist so nothing can get it.

Sometimes I give the mice the tiniest bit.

Lice come to us, too. They're in our hair and in our ears and on our eyelids, moving all the time. They're in our clothes, too, the same clothes we wore when we left the ghetto. They're everywhere, the lice, even in the spaces between our legs.

Mameh squishes the lice in my hair with her fingertips.

You might think that's gross, disgusting. And it is.

But I'm eight years old now, and I know if we weren't inside this haystack — if we were on a road, or in the forest — we'd be killed. I'm more thankful to be alive than upset about the lice.

Tateh says some Ukrainians are hiding Jews for money, but Pavlo wouldn't hide us even one day for money. Pavlo is a religious man, Tateh says. Pavlo doesn't even believe in money. He hates the Soviet Union's Stalin as much as he hates Germany's Hitler.

In the afternoon Pavlo whistles and Brisko comes. Then Pavlo whispers something in Brisko's ear, and Brisko runs out across the fields.

Then we wait.

If we don't hear Brisko barking, we don't do anything.

If we hear Brisko barking I start lacing up my boots.

Brisko is protecting us, like Pavlo.

The other day Brisko only sat and watched, though, when Pavlo told us to come out from the haystack, that it was time for us to leave.

So we crawled out of the haystack, and stood up. We can't stand very straight.

Pavlo picked me up and started to cry. He said I was only a child, that I didn't deserve to die. Then he said it was going to snow, that maybe it wasn't the right time, after all, for us to leave.

So here we are, the three of us, back inside our haystack. We're sitting so close we touch.

When I look at Tateh he looks the same, but he isn't the same. Before, he was always in charge. Before, we never worried about anything. Now Tateh can't even leave our haystack and another man, Pavlo, is bringing us food — mostly potatoes boiled with the skins.

Pavlo carries food to us in the big pockets of a big coat.

Pavlo even empties the pot at night.

We all go the bathroom in the same pot.

When I look at Mameh she looks the same, too, I guess, but she talks less than before. I can't forget the sound her blood made — *zhhh, zhhh, zhhh* — when the *Bandérivtsi* hit her with the fat ends of their guns. They said bullets were too good for Jews. Hanna and I heard them say it.

They hit Mameh so many times she had seven holes in her head. Seven!

They broke her nose. They broke a bone over her eye.

They thought she was dead.

But here she is, next to me, alive. My leg is touching her leg.

Like I said I'm not scared but maybe I'm a little bit afraid.

We don't want our lives to be over. We want to live.

I guess I'm afraid and thankful at the same time.

I'm thankful to Pavlo, most of all.

And I thank God my sister is in our house. I thank God she's in a better place.

The Barn

There's more hay on top of us here, in the barn, than there was in our haystack.

There's so much hay I feel too covered and it's hard to breathe — like that time under the sheet when my father and uncle thought I was dead.

Because it's winter Pavlo dug a ditch for us in the barn so we could live in the barn instead of the field. The ground was too wet, though, too cold. So he filled in the ditch and made another hole for us in the hay, in the barn.

Here, whenever someone wants to turn, everyone has to turn.

Here, we can see out between the boards in a wall.

The whole time we've been at Pavlo's farm we haven't washed ourselves even once. Not even our hands, our faces. Any water we get is enough to wet our tongues.

At night Tateh pulls off a plank of wood from the wall, crawls out, then runs down the hill, to the river, to empty and wash the pot.

You probably think that's the worst, going the bathroom in the same pot as your parents.

If you were me, though — afraid you might die before the next day — would you worry about never changing clothes, or never taking a bath, or always sharing a pot?

I miss Hanna so much. I just really miss my big sister.

When we moved into the barn it was October. It's November now. Tateh keeps count of the days of the week so we can say a prayer on Fridays before we go to bed.

Before the pogrom, before the ghetto, my favorite day was Saturday. Every week I began thinking of Saturday before it was even Saturday. Jews don't work or even cook on Saturdays — the Sabbath. So the day before, on Friday, before it got dark, Hanna and I would carry Mameh's clay pot to the baker and he'd put it in his oven. All the Jews in Tuchin did this.

Inside the pot Mameh put beef, potatoes and onions — sometimes beans, sometimes barley.

The stew, the pot, the whole thing is called a *cholnt*.

On Saturday mornings we'd go to the synagogue, then Hanna and I would go back to the baker's and pick up the *cholnt*. Because it was in the oven all night everything inside turned into a stew. Then we'd carry it home. While we were gone Mameh would cover the table with a white tablecloth.

Then we'd eat, all four of us.

Then we'd take a nap.

After we woke up we'd put on our newest clothes and go for a walk around town to show off our clothes. Mameh bought dresses specially from a dressmaker.

We strolled. That was the word, to stroll.

Like I said Saturday was my favorite day of the week. But now we don't have any favorite days. Whatever day it is we just hope we don't die before the next day.

Stillness

My hair is thicker now, and I can stay
close to my little girl even though
it's colder and colder, and even though
I still don't like to be alone, when
it's just me in my yard, no one else,
I can relax, just really relax, and
I don't even worry when I can't hear
my little girl because I know
she's still there, under the hay,
that she's just better at staying and
being quiet, too, but sometimes I just
can't relax, even when it's just me,
because sometimes the man starts to
whisper too much, and then he starts
to sing, and then the woman and
my little girl start to sing, and even
though they sing quietly I start to
worry, I can't help it, so I start to look
around, and then I start to walk around,
but even though I'm looking and
walking I hardly see anyone, any
people, anymore. Master is keeping

my little girl the same way Master
kept me when I was little, even if
he didn't keep my brothers and sisters.
Now I'm not so little, but my little
girl isn't so little, either. At least
she's not as little as when we first
looked at each other, before
she ever lived in a haystack.

Eighteen Months

I don't know why I'm always tired. For eighteen months I've hardly ever moved — just my legs, really.

Eighteen months is a year and a half.

Tateh tries to make Mameh and me feel less tired by remembering out loud stories from the Hebrew Bible. He knows them by heart.

I can understand him even though I don't speak Hebrew. Whenever I talk I talk in Yiddish.

Tateh also makes us feel less tired by singing songs. Some songs everybody knows, other songs Jews know, like this one —

Al ha-Yam ha-Tichon

Sha-ta sfi-na kala

Vi-digla kachol lavan

Vi-digla kachol lavan

Na na na na na na

Sha-ta sha-ta sha-ta

Na na na na na na

The song says, "On the Mediterranean Sea a little ship is sailing with a blue and white flag, with a blue and white flag — sailing, sailing, sailing."

I've never seen a sea. I've never seen a ship.

The blue and white flag means a safe place for Jews that doesn't exist, yet.

We sing in whispers and we talk in whispers and we remember the Bible, in whispers.

But we don't laugh anymore, not even in whispers.

None of us laughs. Never, ever.

Some days Tateh carves shoes from wood for Pavlo and his family. Some days Mameh knits dresses and sweaters for Lyubka and the girls. But most days we only sit and sit.

I don't know what Mameh and Tateh are thinking when they look out between the boards, but when I look out and see a bird I wish I were a bird, too — that I could fly away.

My God, to be a bird!

Almost every time I look out I see Brisko.

Brisko stays close to me — even when it's cold and snowy, like now.

I love Brisko even though I've never petted him.

Not even once.

When I look out I know I don't want anything, anymore. Any things, I mean.

I don't want a house, or jewelry, or new clothes.

I only want to sit outside, on the bench, near the barn.

I only want to sit there, though, if no one will be mean to me because I'm Jewish.

44

Actually, more than anything I want to be with Hanna. But the next thing I want is to sit, unafraid, on the bench.

The other day Pavlo told us to come out from under the hay, that this time it was really time for us to leave. My parents crawled out but they couldn't stand up. I didn't have to try to stand up because Pavlo picked me up, instead.

Pavlo held me in his arms. Then he began to cry.

He shouldn't have picked me up because after that he couldn't make us go.

So now we're back in the barn, under the hay.

My parents say Pavlo never wanted to keep us, but he got stuck.

Pavlo doesn't have the heart to make us go.

Actually, Pavlo has too much heart.

If it weren't for Pavlo, we'd be dead. He brings us whatever food he can, and whatever food he brings us is food he isn't bringing his own family.

Pavlo is like a god to us. That's what we call him, "Our god."

He's getting skinny. He's like a stick.

The Horsemen

It's dark and I'm alone in my yard
when I hear hooves, horses' hooves,
on the dirt road near my farm,
and before I even know it the hair
on my back is sticking up, and
my ears are back, and my tail is low,
and I'm standing up except I don't
know where to stand because
my little girl is in the barn,
but Master is in the house, and
before I can even choose the horses
are in the yard, and there are men
on the horses, and it's just me
and the horses and the men,
but then Master is in the yard, too,
and now my teeth are showing, and
noise is coming out of my mouth,
and I'm shaking all over, and

I don't even try to stop any of this
from happening because all I want
is for the horses and the men
to go away, but they're not going
away, the men are just talking
to Master, and Master is just
talking to the men, and they keep
talking and talking and before
I even know it the noise isn't
coming out of my mouth anymore,
and my hair isn't sticking up
anymore, and even though
I like to hear people talking,
this time, I don't.

Unexpected Visitors

We were sleeping when Brisko began to bark and bark.

I thought, "Oh my God! Who's coming?"

I began to lace my boots.

Now my boots are laced and Brisko still won't stop barking.

Between the boards I see Pavlo in the moonlight.

He's talking — talking with Nazis, on horses.

Tateh whispers to Mameh that the Nazis didn't come from the west, from Germany. He whispers that they came from the east, from where they were fighting the Soviets.

I start to ask a question but Tateh covers my mouth with his hand.

"They're going home," he says.

If the Nazis are going home, he says, that means maybe the Nazis are losing the war. And if the Nazis are losing, then World War II might be ending — and soon we might be able to go home, too, to live again together, with Hanna, in our dream house.

Out of all the farms around Tuchin why did the Nazis choose this one?

And why is Pavlo pointing them toward our barn?

Like Out of a Book

The Nazis are still here, in the barn.

They're on the top of our hay, and we're on the bottom.

The Nazis are so close I can hear the sounds of their cigarettes as they smoke.

I can't tell how many there are. Eight, maybe? Ten?

They've been here for twelve days, I think.

I don't really know how long they've been here, though. Since they came Tateh stopped counting out loud the days.

Since they came I haven't sneezed, or coughed, or snored.

Since they came we haven't emptied the pot.

We're hungry, we're thirsty. But all we do is sit all day with the mice, and the lice.

Now it's really like I'm reading about my life in a book.

Pavlo is smart. He told the Nazis to move their horses into the barn even though they didn't want to move in with their horses. That way the Nazis will think any sounds we make are being made by their horses.

Pavlo moved Brisko closer to us, too — tied him outside the barn.

We know that if the Nazis find us we'll be killed.

We also know that if the Nazis don't find us we might be killed — if Pavlo makes us leave.

It's winter, 1943, and we can't believe we're still alive.

We wonder if maybe we're the only Jews left in the whole world.

Goodbyes

Master untied me as soon as they left,
the horses and the men, and the first
thing I did was shake all over, and
shake some more, then I walked
to where they peed, the men, and
I peed where they peed, and I did it
the next moon, and the next moon,
until I could only smell myself,
not them, and even though I didn't
have to stay in one place anymore
my little girl still did, she didn't
come out from under the hay,
she just stayed and stayed until today,
when Master opened the barn door
and held it open, and the man came out,
and the woman came out, and then
my little girl came out, my little girl,
and it took them so long to come out,
just so so long, and the whole time
they were coming out Master
was holding open the door, and
then we were all there, together,

in my yard, and we all just looked
at each other, not talking, just looking,
then Master gave something to the man,
and the man gave it back, then Master
finally talked, and the man finally took
the thing Master gave him, then Master
gave the man something else, and then
the man finally talked, and the whole
time they were giving and taking and
talking my little girl was looking at me,
and I was looking at her, and we were
still looking at each other when the man
began to walk, and the woman began
to walk, which was when my heart
began to go really, really fast, because
the woman took my little girl by the hand
and my little girl began to walk, too,
and they all kept walking, just like that,
and the whole time they were walking
Master and I were watching, not moving,
in my yard, just watching them as they
walked down the hill, toward the river,
and even though I looked and looked
my little girl didn't once look back.

Liberation

Hanna is dead.

We know because Ukrainians in Tuchin know, and they told my father.

After the ghetto was set on fire, and Nazis were killed by Jews, the Nazis were so angry that the principal's wife got scared and told Hanna to leave our house. One of Hanna's classmates from school saw her outside, pointed at her.

Hanna wouldn't say where she had been, or where she was going. So she was beaten, and tortured, and killed.

Hanna died on November 4, 1942.

She was eleven years old.

The whole time we were under the hay we thought she was alive — in our house, on the other side of the river. But the whole time we were thinking of her she was already dead.

If my parents hadn't let her go she would still be with us.

If it weren't for our house — our dream house — Hanna would still be alive.

My parents and I were liberated on January 16, 1944. That's the word, to liberate. It means that the

Soviets came through Tuchin on January 16 while they were chasing the Nazis back to Germany. And then we were free.

Even though we were free Pavlo wouldn't let us leave. For three more weeks he told us to stay where we were, in the barn, under the hay.

I didn't understand.

My parents told me that even though the Nazis were gone, the Ukrainians weren't. And some Ukrainians were killing Jews because of bad things they did — the Ukrainians — during the war.

I still didn't understand.

Jews are witnesses, they told me. Jews saw lots of the bad things Ukrainians did because lots of the bad things were done to Jews. And because Ukrainians who did bad things don't want other people to know what they did, they've been killing Jews who survived — like us — when they return to their homes.

That way there aren't as many witnesses.

I guess maybe I understand, but understanding makes me afraid.

I'm a witness. Mameh and Tateh are witnesses.

I don't like it when I hear German. But when I hear Ukrainian, I shiver.

Tateh says there were three thousand Jews in the Tuchin ghetto. Now there are twelve Jews in the whole town. That's nine people, plus us.

We want to live how we lived before, but we can't live how we lived before.

Life has changed too much.

The day Pavlo said it was safe enough to come out from under the hay I already knew it was safe because Brisko hardly ever barked anymore.

We crawled into the yard, and stood up. My parents couldn't stand up without falling over so they put their hands on the outside of the barn.

We stood quietly in the yard. I looked long at Brisko, and he looked long at me.

Pavlo wanted to give Mameh's watch to Tateh, but Tateh wouldn't take it. Then Pavlo said we had to take it so we could sell it for money, to live.

So Tateh took it.

Then Pavlo gave us some food, also to live.

Pavlo is our god.

We're not allowed to tell anyone that Pavlo hid us during the war. If some Ukrainians knew they would burn down his farm — or hurt him, or his wife, or their children.

Then Tateh started to walk, and Mameh started to walk. Because Mameh gave me her hand, I took it, and I started to walk, too.

My parents used long sticks to stop from falling over but by the time we were close to Tuchin all three of us were crawling, not walking. We didn't care that we were crawling because the more we crawled, the closer we got to Hanna.

We didn't know she was dead.

I still have dirt under my fingernails from crawling.

When we got to Tuchin the Soviets told us we couldn't live in our house even though the principal and his wife were gone. They told us all Jews had to live in the same house, a house across the road from the police station.

We're safer that way, they said — safer from the Ukrainians.

Our house isn't our dream house, anymore.

Tuchin isn't even Tuchin, anymore.

It's still called Tuchin, but my relatives are dead and the poor part of town, where they put the ghetto, is all burned and black. The big pot in the hole in our basement is gone. My diploma and my dolly are gone.

We don't want to live in this Tuchin.

All my parents talk about is leaving — moving to a place where we can trust our neighbors.

We can't move anywhere, yet, because we're all sick. We all have typhoid fever.

I'm so sick Mameh shaved my head, and now my straight hair is growing back curly.

Tateh says two thousand Jews ran away from the ghetto during the fire. The rest of the people, one thousand, died before the ghetto even stopped burning. But almost all the people who ran away from the ghetto died, too. They were found and killed in the forests.

Some of the people who ran away, the mothers with babies, couldn't stay long in the forests. So they walked out of the forests, back to Tuchin, where they were killed — the mothers and babies.

It's hard for me to imagine all the Jews who died in Tuchin even though I'm almost ten years old.

I don't feel as little as my age.

I don't feel like I'm reading about my life in a book anymore, either. I know it's all true.

My parents and I keep telling each other it's a miracle we survived.

It's all miracles, really. Miracles of miracles.

About Laura Oberlender

Laura Oberlender

Lyubov Khomut was born in Tuchin on August 5, 1934, when the town was still part of Poland. This photograph — a rare memento from Lyuba's life prior to the Holocaust — shows Lyuba in the lower right with her older sister, Hanna, and the girls' maternal grandmother, Dvara.

After the war, in a displaced persons camp, Lyuba and her parents changed their names: Lyuba became Laura Emmet.

After the family immigrated to the United States, Laura again changed her name: In 1955 she took the last name of her husband, Alex Oberlender.

Today Lyubov Khomut is known as Laura Oberlender.

Laura Oberlender in the spring of 2018

Paul Dempsey

Laura and Alex, a Jew from Czechoslovakia who also survived the Holocaust, lived in Philadelpha, Pennsylvania. They had three children: Randie, Susan, and Steven. After Alex died in 1987, Laura moved to Atlantic City, New Jersey. There she eventually met Ernest Paul, also a Holocaust survivor from Czechoslovakia. In 2013, Laura and Ernest married. In 2016, Ernest died. Laura lives in New Jersey during the summer, and in Florida during the winter. She has six grandchildren, all girls.

About Pirl and Isaak

Laura Oberlender

This photo of Pirl and Isaak Khomut is undated, but predates the Holocaust. After returning to Tuchin from Pavlo's farm, the couple — Isaak was facing conscription into the Soviet Red Army — made their way, with Lyuba, to the nearby city of Rivne. Then, as warplanes fought in skies overhead, they made their way to Lodz, Poland, before reaching a displaced persons camp in Linz, Austria.

The Khomuts lived at the camp for more than three years. There, Pirl gave birth to a son, Michael, and the family changed last names: the Khomuts became Emmets.

The couple long had hoped to resettle in the former British territory of Palestine. In 1949, however, the Emmets instead immigrated to the U.S. city of Philadelphia, Pennsylvania.

Pirl died in in 1989 at the age of 85, and Isaak died in 1996 at the age of 94.

About Pavlo Gerasimchik

Yad Vashem

In 1990 Pavlo and his wife, Lyubka, were recognized as Righteous Among the Nations by Yad Vashem, the Holocaust Martyrs' and Heroes' Remembrance Authority, for risking their own lives to save the lives of Lyuba and her parents. In 1999 Pavlo's children — Klavdiya (Kucheruk), Halina (Galina) Gavrishchuk, and Mykola (Nikolai) Gerasimchik — were also recognized by Yad Vashem as Righteous Among the Nations.

Yad Vashem

Pavlo and his family pose in front of the farmhouse in which Laura and her mother lived, briefly, in the attic. Pavlo's wife, Lyubka, is wearing a headscarf in the second row, center. Also in the second row are the couple's son, Mykola (Nikolai), and, to Lyubka's left, daughters Halina (Galina) and Klavdiya, respectively. The dog in the foreground is believed to be Brisko.

The identities of the other people in the photo are unknown.

Pavlo and Lyubka pose before the barn where Lyuba and her parents hid, and where German soldiers lived while in retreat. In the upper right is a haystack similar to the one in which the Khomuts initially hid in a field on Pavlo's farm.

About Brisko

The dog in this photo is believed to be Brisko, but no one — not even Laura — knows for sure.

One need not be able to speak to have a voice.

Tuchin During the Holocaust

On July 6, 1941, units of the German 6th Army occupied Tuchin.* In the first days — accounts vary as to the exact date — antisemitic Ukrainians staged a pogrom, looting houses and killing an estimated 60 to 70 Jews. The day after the pogrom German forces, using lists drawn up by Ukrainians, arrested and shot to death 20 Jews, plus five Ukrainians alleged to be Communists and Soviet activists.

Over the summer, and into fall, the town's estimated 2,600 Jews were required to wear armbands (later, a yellow patch) bearing an image of the Star of David. Jews were forbidden from leaving town limits; some were conscripted into forced labor, such as making clothes for German soldiers.

During this period Ukrainian police systematically robbed and beat Jews. German authorities also seized valuables from Jews, including livestock — resulting in food shortages.

Some non-Jews stopped acknowledging their Jewish friends and acquaintances.

For more than a year Jews in Tuchin lived in a form of open ghetto — they could come, and go, within town limits — because the local Jewish Council, or *Judenrat*, bribed German authorities. But bribes weren't enough to stop the formal creation of a ghetto in early September 1942.

In ensuing weeks Jews from Tuchin and surrounding areas — some 3,000 people overall — were crowded into about 50 small houses along one street. Many slept on floors.

By then Jews in Tuchin had heard about the mass murder of Jews in nearby Rivne. So when Jews in Tuchin learned that Germans were digging mass graves nearby, they decided to resist.

Plans spearheaded by Judenrat members Hershel Schwarzman and Meir Himmelfarb called upon Jews in the Tuchin ghetto to set fire to houses and German warehouses as soon as German soldiers and Ukrainian police moved to kill them. Not only that, some Jews would meet the advancing soldiers and police with gunfire — providing cover so other Jews could escape into the surrounding forests.

Judenrat funds were spent on kerosene with which to start the fires, as well as weapons, including at least five rifles and more than 20 revolvers.

On September 21, 1942 — three days before the ghetto was slated to be liquidated — Schwarzman and other leaders of the resistance revealed their plans to other Jews who had gathered to pray together on the Jewish high holiday of Yom Kippur, or Day of Atonement.

Two days later, on the evening of September 23, forces of the German Security Police (Sipo) and Security Service (SD), assisted by German Gendarmerie and Ukrainian police, surrounded the ghetto.

At dawn on September 24, the armed forces attacked the ghetto and the people inside.

Jewish resisters set fire to buildings, as planned, then opened fire on the advancing forces. Other Jews in the ghetto fled amid the chaos — breaking through, and climbing over, wooden barriers.

The uprising lasted for three days.

By the end of the third day, on September 26, about 1,000 Jews had been killed. Several Germans and Ukrainians also had been killed, or wounded. Among the Jewish dead were many of the resisters, including Schwarzman and Himmelfarb.

About 2,000 Jews — including many women and children — reached the forests.

Germans and Ukrainian police organized a manhunt to capture the Jews who escaped. Within several days about half of the Jews who escaped had been captured, and killed. Jews who realized they would not survive in the forests, primarily women and children, returned to Tuchin, where they were shot and killed.

During the fall of 1942, Soviet records show:

Some 753 Jews were executed in the Jewish cemetery in Tuchin; some 240 Jews were killed by Ukrainian nationalist partisans in the Kudrinka Forest; and more than 300 Jews, Poles and Ukrainians were shot and killed by German Gendarmerie in the town park.

While some Jews survived through winter in the forests, many died of hunger and cold.

Some Jews — like Lyuba's sister, Hanna — were denounced to Germans or killed by Ukrainians. (A few of the younger Jewish escapees eventually joined Soviet partisan fighting units.)

Only around 20 Jews in and around Tuchin survived until liberation on January 16, 1944.

* Tuchin is the predominant English-language spelling — transliterated from Russian — from the Soviet period, when the town was part of the Ukrainian Soviet Socialist Republic. Today the town commonly is spelled Tuchyn, the transliteration from Ukrainian.

(Source: United States Holocaust Memorial Museum *Encyclopedia of Camps and Ghettos, 1933-1945*)

Acknowledgments

Laura Oberlender and her late husband, Ernest Paul, welcomed me into their home more times, surely, than they ever anticipated. Laura listened patiently to my questions, and entrusted me with her answers. When I pushed deeper into moments from her childhood, she answered matter-of-factly; if there was something she didn't remember, or remembered diffferently from others, so be it.

Each time, before walking me to the door, Laura made sure I took candy, for the road.

I learned of Laura only because Peter Murphy learned that the Sara and Sam Schoffer Holocaust Resource Center, at Stockton University, knew of a Holocaust survivor living in Atlantic City who needed help telling her story. I didn't yet know the survivor, or her story, but I knew she had a wish: that her story would be taught in schools, and that schools would invite her to meet with students.

As a former Moscow-based correspondent who reported from post-Soviet Ukraine, I knew how tricky it can be to write about history from a part of the world where events that happened years ago — even hundreds of years ago — can be looked upon as if they happened yesterday. Jared McBride shared what he knew about violence during World War II in western Ukraine, and steered me to resources that helped reassure me I did all I could to get things right.

I know Russian and some Ukrainian, but I don't know Hebrew or Yiddish. Nili Keren translated a map of Tuchin during the war, while Danna Paz Prins and Rabbi Sarah Cohen, separately, translated (and transliterated) the lyrics of the song Laura sang, with her parents, under the hay. Lyudmila Sholokhova connected me to people, and resources, in an effort to trace the song's origins.

An early draft of Laura's story benefited from a critique by members of the Backyard Writers Workshop, in Philadelphia, specifically: Alisha Ebling, Sara Graybeal, Susanna Greenberg, Patrick McNeil, David Poplar, Elias Rodriques, and Lorine Kimball Vogt. Subsequent drafts benefited from close reads by: Frank Brown, Savva Brown, Karen Z. Duffy, Stephen Dunn, Sandy Gingras, Barbara Hurd, Catherine Lord, Diane MacWilliams, Erika MacWilliams, Jared McBride, Peter Murphy, Doreen Rappaport, Josephine von Zitzewitz, and Venise Wagner.

Raz Segal helped clear the path to publication when it appeared the book might never reach readers. Renée Ashley guided me to Walter Cummins, who offered the book a home. Along the path timely feedback and direction (and connection) was provided by: Murl Barker, Barbara Daniels, Isabel De Sousa, Lawrence Glaser, Ken Kalfus, Yuliya Komska, Valerie Linson, Daniel Magilow, Ian Mellanby, Ronald Miller, Frances Osugi, Ethan Pollock, Colleen Tambuscio, and Kara Wentworth.

At the United States Holocaust Memorial Museum in Washington, D.C., Vadim Altskan and Geoffrey Megargee ensured I had permission to adapt the entry on Tuchin from the museum's *Encyclopedia of Camps and Ghettos, 1933-1945*. At Yad Vashem in Israel, Irena Steinfeldt provided me with digital copies of photographs of Pavlo, his family, and their dog, Brisko.

About the Author

Bryon MacWilliams is an American writer whose memoir, *With Light Steam: A Personal Journey through the Russian Baths,* was published in 2014 to good reviews. He won awards for his reporting at U.S. daily newspapers before moving in 1996 to Moscow, where he was based for nearly twelve years as a foreign correspondent reporting from the territories of the former Soviet Union. His journalism, essays, poetry, and literary translations have appeared in anthologies and numerous other publications, including: *The New York Times, The Chronicle of Higher Education, The Philadelphia Inquirer, The Literary Review,* B O D Y, *Solstice, Nature,* and *Science.*